M000158402

Purple Ronnie's

Little Poems for

FRIENDS

First published 1999 by Boxtree
an imprint of PanMacmillan Publishers Ltd.
20 New Wharf Road
London N1 9RR

www.panmacmillan.com

Associated companies throughout the world

ISBN 0 7522 17283

19 18

A CIP catalogue record for this book is
available from the British Library

Text by Giles Andreae
Illustrations by Janet Cronin
Printed and bound in Hong Kong

a poem about

Good Friends

When you've got friends
you can talk to
You don't have to try to be
clever
It's so much more fun
To sit down on your bum
And go through your love
lives together

a poem about
Missing You

There are times when I
 really do miss you
And think of you missing me
 too
So I close my eyes tight
And I daydream
That I am together with you

lovely daydream

a shy poem

To Someone I Like

I sometimes find it rather
hard
To say I really care
And that I like you quite
a lot,
But I've said it now —
so there

a poem about

Friends

Some people think that
it's great to be rich

To be cool and keep up with
the trends

But riches and looks just
don't matter at all

Cos what really counts is your
friends

a poem about a
Huggle

A huggle is something you
share with a friend

You can huggle in all kinds
of ways

Huggling makes you feel
all sort of warm

And perfectly splendid for
days

a poem called ↓

Thinking of You

I'm thinking of you lots
and lots

So here's what I can do

I'm sending loads of
happy vibes

And friendly thoughts
to you

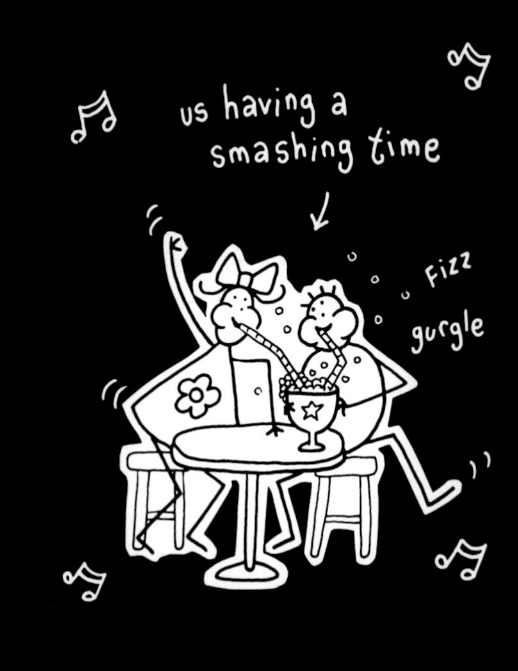
us having a
smashing time
Fizz
gurgle

a poem about ↓

My Friend

A friend is a person who
helps you to laugh
And makes you feel happy
and free
A friend is the grooviest
thing you can have
A friend is what you are
to ME

a poem about
↓
My Little Plan

The fact that you're so
smashing
Made me hatch a little
Plan
I wanted just to tell you
I'm your all-time
greatest fan

a poem saying

↓

I Like You

You tell me I'm fat and
I'm ugly
You tell me I'm utterly nuts
You tell me I burp and I fart
and I smell
But that's why I like you
so much

a poem about a

Cuddle Token

I've got you something
wonderful
That can't be smashed
or broken
I hope you use it lots
'Cos it's my special Cuddle
Token

a poem to say

You're Special

You're a very special person

And you mean a lot to me

When you're around you
make the world

A better place to be

a poem to say

You Make Me Happy

Sometimes I close my eyes
tightly
And dream of you while
you're away
Cos thinking of you makes
me happy
So that's what I wanted
to say

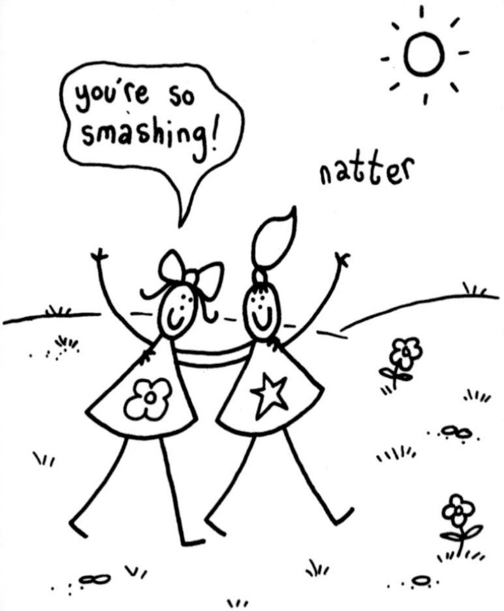
you're so smashing!
natter

a poem about
↓
Being Friends

If you need some cheering
up
Because you're sad or blue

Or you need someone to
talk to

I'll be always there for you

Friend_aly Poem

Never think twice about
calling me up
To say that your pride has
been dented
To tell me you're happy or
lonely or sad
'Cos that is why friends
were invented

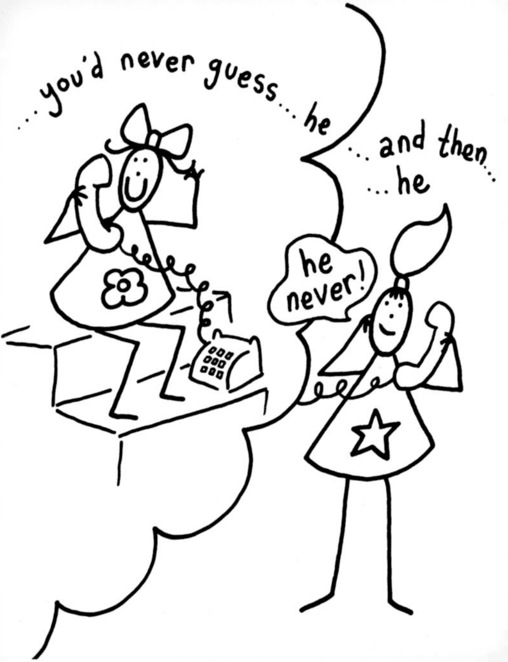
...you'd never guess...he
...and then...
...he
he never!

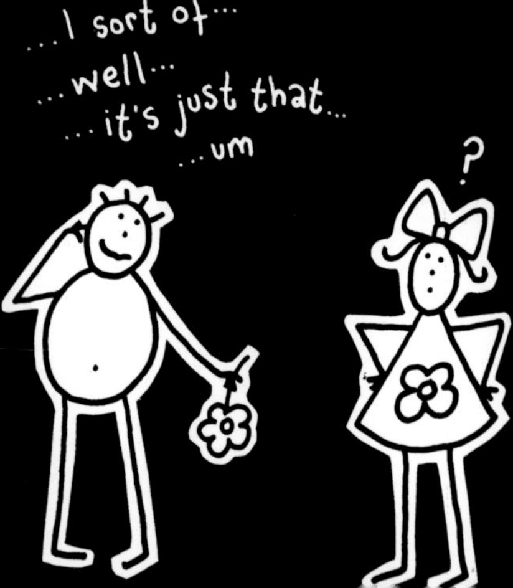
...I sort of...
...well...
...it's just that...
...um
?

a poem about
↓

My Own Little Way

I sometimes get rather
embarrassed

And don't always know
what to say

When it comes to expressing
my feelings

But I try in my own little
way

a lovely
Hugging Poem

I want you to know
That I think you are great
And although I'm a bit of
a mug
If you ever need me
I'll always be near
To come round and give you
a hug

...and when they do your bikini line...
ooh! the pain!
wince
shudder
FAB SHOES

a poem for a

GOSSIP

What it is we talk
about

Really doesn't matter

As long as we can just
sit down

And have a good old
natter

a poem for a

Lovely Person

Has anyone recently told
you
How totally lovely you are?
If not here's a poem to
tell you
That this person thinks
you're a star

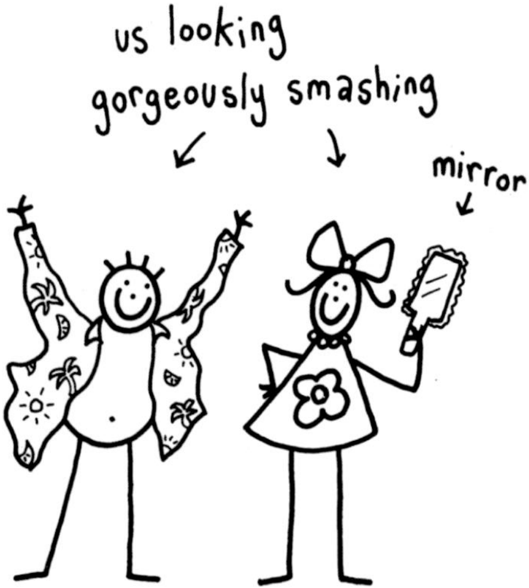
us looking
gorgeously smashing
mirror

☆ a poem for a ☆
↓
Gorgeously
Smashing Person

However much money I
pay people
Some of them still won't
agree
That you're almost as
wonderfully scrumptious
And gorgeously smashing as
me

a poem for

My Groovy Mate

Thanks for being so groovy

Thanks for being so great

Thanks for being so totally
fab

Thanks for being my
mate

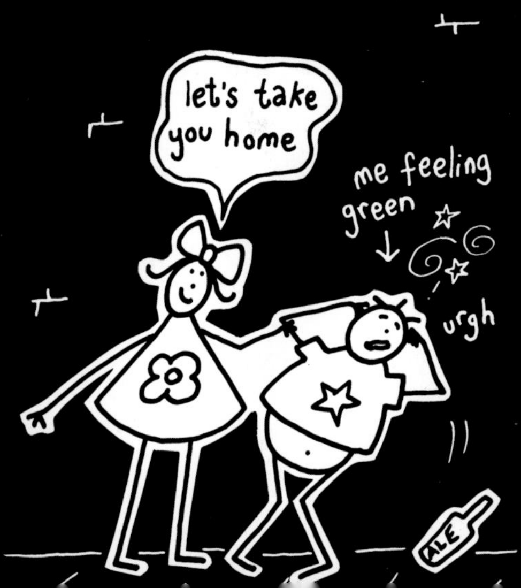
let's take you home
me feeling green
urgh
ALE

a poem for an

Extra Special Person

If I had a million pounds

I know what I would do

I'd buy some extra
        special times

And spend them all
        with you

a poem to say

You're Lovely

If I was more clever
I would find a special way
To tell you that you're
                    lovely
Cos that's all I want
                to say